THE TEN CC

MW01528196

Written

Illustrations: *Daniel Canlas*

TABLE OF CONTENTS

ISBN 978-1-936020-32-4

THE BIRTH OF MOSES

God created us to share His love with us! However, our first parents disobeyed God and turned away from Him. Yet God did not turn away from them. He promised to send a Redeemer who would save us from our sins.

God chose Abraham to be the father of His chosen people, the Hebrews, who were also called the Israelites. The Hebrews went to Egypt, where God provided for them during a great famine. At first the Egyptians were kind to them, but then they made them their slaves. A cruel ruler, the Pharaoh, was afraid that the Hebrews would become more powerful than his own people. Therefore he made them work harder, and he ordered all Hebrew baby boys to be drowned in the Nile River.

A Hebrew woman gave birth to a son, whom she loved very much. She hid her baby at home, but when he was three months old she put him in a little basket in the river and sent his sister, Miriam, to secretly watch over him.

The daughter of the Pharaoh came to the river to bathe, and she discovered the little basket floating in the river! She decided to keep the baby. Miriam offered to have her mother nurse the baby. The Pharaoh's daughter named the little boy Moses, meaning "saved out of the water."

MOSES AND THE BURNING BUSH

Moses grew up in the Pharaoh's palace, but he never forgot that he was an Israelite. When he was 40 years old, Moses killed an Egyptian for striking a Hebrew slave. Pharaoh heard of it and wanted to put Moses to death, so Moses fled to Arabia, where he became a shepherd.

One day, while Moses was tending his sheep, God appeared to him in a burning bush. Moses was surprised that the bush did not burn up, and so he went nearer to see it. God called, "Moses! Moses!" He answered, "Here I am." God told Moses to come no nearer until he had removed his sandals, for he was standing on holy ground. "I am the God of your father," God said, "the God of Abraham, Isaac, and Jacob. I have seen the burden of my people Israel and I have come down to rescue them from the Egyptians and lead them into the Promised Land. I will send you to Pharaoh to lead my people out of Egypt."

God promised to be with Moses. He told him to throw down his staff, and it became a snake. Then he threw it down again, and it changed back into a staff. God told Moses to use his staff to help the people believe that God had appeared to him. God also said He would send Aaron, Moses' brother, to help him to free the Hebrews from Egypt.

THE PASSOVER OF THE LORD

Moses and Aaron went to the Pharaoh and said, "God tells you: 'Let My people go!'" But the Pharaoh would not obey God. Therefore God sent nine different plagues upon the land of Egypt, but still the Pharaoh would not let the Hebrews go. He only made them work harder.

Before sending the tenth and final plague, God commanded Moses to tell each Hebrew family to sacrifice a special lamb. He told them to apply some of the blood of the lamb on their doorposts. He told them to eat the lamb that night with unleavened bread. It was the Passover of the Lord.

That same night the angel of the Lord visited the houses of Egypt that were not marked with the blood of the lamb. In every home that was not marked with the blood, the angel of the Lord put to death every first born male of man or beast, in the whole land of Egypt.

There was great sorrow in the whole land of Egypt. The Egyptians wept loudly, because everywhere there was death, from the house of the poorest family in Egypt to the palace of the Pharaoh.

THE EXODUS

Pharaoh arose that same night, called Moses and Aaron, and said to them, "Leave my people at once, you and the Israelites with you! Go and worship the Lord as you said. Take your flocks of sheep, too, and your herds of cattle, and be gone; and you will be doing me a favor." The Israelites then departed Egypt that night, without even time to bake any bread.

God led the Israelites out of Egypt, going before them as a cloud by day and a pillar of fire by night. Pharaoh was sorry he had let the Hebrews go, so he took his army, his horses, and his chariots, and went off to capture the Israelites and bring them back. By now the Hebrews had reached the Red Sea. Moses told the people, "Do not be afraid! Stand your ground, and you will see the victory that the Lord will win for you today."

Moses stretched out his hand over the sea, and the waters parted. Then all the people crossed over to the other side. Moses then stretched out his hand over the sea, and the waters returned back to their place. As the waters flowed back, they covered Pharaoh's whole army, his chariots and charioteers. When Israel saw the great power of God, they believed in him and in his servant Moses. God had delivered His people from the land of Egypt!

GOD GIVES MOSES
THE TEN COMMANDMENTS

God had set His people free from Egypt so that they could worship Him. Three months after leaving Egypt, the Israelites came to Mount Sinai. God called Moses to the mountain and told him to tell the people that if they remained faithful to the Lord, He would continue to protect them and would make them His very own chosen people. God also commanded the people to prepare themselves for two days, so as to be ready for the third day, for on the third day the Lord would come down on Mount Sinai in the sight of all the people.

On the morning of the third day, thunder and lightening began to break out in the heavens. A thick cloud covered the mountain, and the top of Mount Sinai looked as if were on fire! After that came the sound of a trumpet blast, growing louder and louder until the people trembled with fear.

Then the Lord God Himself came down to the top of Mount Sinai, and when He had done so, he summoned Moses to the top of the mountain. Then God delivered to Moses the Ten Commandments.

THE FIRST COMMANDMENT

I am the Lord your God.
You shall not have other gods besides Me.

There is only one God. He revealed Himself through
Abraham and Moses and the Jewish prophets as the Creator
of the heavens and the earth. He created all things simply by
speaking His Word.

Jesus revealed to us that this one God is actually a family of
three Persons. The first Person of the Blessed Trinity is God
our heavenly Father, who created everything. The Second
Person is Jesus, the Son of God. He is the Word of God, and
God created everything through His Son. Their love for each
other is the Holy Spirit, who is the Third Person of the
Blessed Trinity.

After Adam and Eve fell away from God, the devil tempted
them to forget God and to worship things that were not God.
This is wrong. God alone is our Father in heaven. He loves us
totally. He gives us everything. He wants us to be with Him
forever in heaven. We are to worship only God, and to serve
Him. Let us obey God, and worship Him alone.

THE SECOND COMMANDMENT

You shall not take the name of the LORD, your God, in vain.

God is a great God, and He is very good and merciful toward all of His creation. Long ago, God appeared to Moses in a burning bush. Moses took off his sandals and bowed low before God. God told Moses He had chosen him to deliver His people Israel out of slavery in Egypt. Moses said, "When the Israelites ask me what is the name of the God of our fathers, what shall I tell them?" God answered, "I am who am" (Exodus 3:14).

When God revealed His Name to Moses, He revealed who He was. Thus we need to respect God's name and to speak of Him with reverence and love. We also need to respect the name of Jesus, the Son of God. Jesus saved us and has come to live in our hearts. Therefore we must not swear using God's name, as this boy is doing. He is saying, "As God is my witness, I did not steal a kite from you!"

We must also not use God's name in a curse or in anger. We must keep God's name holy, as He is holy. May the name of God always be safe in our mouth.

THE THIRD COMMANDMENT

Remember to keep holy the Sabbath day.

On the seventh day, the Sabbath day, God rested from all His work of creation. The Sabbath is made for us, a sacred day on which we are to rest and honor God.

As Catholics, we honor God on Sunday by worshipping Him at Holy Mass. We go with our family to church, which is God's House. In church we join with many other families to praise God as His family, the Body of Christ.

The priest represents Jesus Christ among us at Mass, as he leads us to the altar of God. We tell God we are sorry for our sins, we praise Him, and we listen to His Word in the Readings and in the Gospel. We offer our gifts to God, and then the priest changes our gifts of bread and wine into the Body and Blood of Jesus. If we are old enough, we can receive Jesus in Holy Communion. If not, we can receive Him in our hearts. Finally, the priest sends us out to love God and to love one another.

We must not work on Sundays, if possible. Instead we are to rest and to enjoy this day with our families and loved ones.

THE FOURTH COMMANDMENT

Honor your father and your mother.

God loves families! He gave us our mothers and fathers because He wanted them to love us and care for us, and He wants us to love them as well.

When Jesus was a boy, he loved his father, Saint Joseph, and his mother, Mary. Jesus showed his love by obeying his parents and by helping them.

God wants all of us to love our parents as Jesus did. He wants us to honor them, to obey them, and to help them now and when they are older. In a special way, our parents take God's place on the earth. They provide a home for us. They give us food and clothing, and provide for many of our needs and wants. Our parents teach us about life and help us grow to be adults someday. They are there for us whatever happens, and they watch over us as we grow.

Our parents teach us and send us to school where we learn so much about ourselves and the world which God has given us. Let us obey our parents and listen to their words. Let us honor our father and our mother.

THE FIFTH COMMANDMENT

You shall not kill.

God is the creator of all life. The Scripture says, "Know that the LORD is God, It is he that made us, and we are his" (Psalm 100:3). God loves life and He wants us, His children, to care for all living things. God especially commands us to care for our own life and to care for the lives of others.

We obey the Fifth Commandment when we take care of our bodies. We need to eat our meals, to do our schoolwork, to play and exercise, and to get a good sleep every night. This will help us to feel good and grow up to be healthy adults.

We disobey this commandment when we hurt others or ourselves in any way. We must not hate anyone, although we may feel angry toward them. We must not try to get even with someone by injuring them. We must not fight with others or encourage others to fight.

We must speak only what is true about others. Let us ask Jesus and Mary to help us do good to others always.

THE SIXTH COMMANDMENT

You shall not commit adultery.

It is God's plan that His children be born into families and live in families. A husband and wife have a very special love for one another that they alone can share. It is called a married love. God commands every husband and wife to share this love with each other only.

Fathers and mothers who love each other and obey God keep themselves for each other, and do not give their special love to anyone else. In this way they protect their marriage, and they protect their family. These parents help God, for they carry out His plan and help bring happiness to their families.

God wants us to keep ourselves pure, because we belong to Him. He wants us to speak words that are good and pure. He wants us to look at pictures, books, and shows that are pure. He commands us to avoid any images or books that are impure. A good way to remain pure is to attend Mass often and to receive Jesus in Holy Communion. It is also very good to go to Confession every month. Ask Our Blessed Mother Mary and good Saint Joseph to help you remain pure and full of joy!

THE SEVENTH COMMANDMENT

You shall not steal.

God loves you! He loves every single person in this whole world! He cares for each one of us, and wants each one of us to have enough food to eat and a place to live. He promises to provide for us.

God commands us to use only what is ours, and not to take what belongs to someone else. We need to take good care of what we have. We also need to respect the property of other people. We must not steal anything. If we do take something, we need to give it back right away, and ask God and the person to forgive us. Likewise, if someone we know wants to steal something, we need to remind them that stealing is wrong. Jesus tells us to ask God for what we need, and to trust that God will give it to us, in His time.

God wants us to share the good things we have with other people. If we see someone who is hungry or thirsty, it is good to ask our parents if we can help that person. One way to do this is to put some money into the poor box at church when you can. In this way you help to feed others, and you help them avoid the temptation to steal. Give, and it shall be given to you!

THE EIGHTH COMMANDMENT

You shall not bear false witness against your neighbor.

God is true. God never lies to us. He sent His Son Jesus to speak the truth to us, and He wants us also to always tell the truth. It is hard sometimes to tell the truth, especially when we have done something wrong. However, God understands, and He will help us if we ask Him.

It is good to tell the good things we know about someone else. It is wrong to lie about someone else or say things about him or her that are not true. When we do that we hurt the other person and we also hurt their reputation. God does not want this. He wants each one of us to respect ourselves and to respect others. He wants us to love one another.

It takes courage to tell the truth, because sometimes we may get punished for doing something wrong. But even so, God will be with us. When we tell a lie, we may be able to fool other people for a time, but we know inside ourselves that we have not told the truth. However, when we do tell the truth, even when it is hard, we can be at peace because we are not trying to deceive anyone. We are true to God, to ourselves, and to others. We are free!

THE NINTH COMMANDMENT

You shall not covet your neighbor's wife.

To "covet" means to want or to desire something. In this commandment God instructs husbands to be happy with their own wives. He tells them not to look for someone else's wife to make them happy.

God knows what we need. In the Sermon on the Mount, Jesus told us, "Consider the birds of the air; they neither sow nor reap nor gather into barns, yet your heavenly Father feeds them. Are you not worth much more than many sparrows?" (Matthew 6:26). Think about all the birds and the other living creatures on the earth. They all live because God feeds them, and makes food available for them in many different and wonderful ways.

In the same way, Jesus tells us that God will provide for us, who are His children. Therefore we do not have to covet or look for what belongs to someone else. God will take good care of us.

God commands all people to be pure. If an impure thought comes to your mind, bring it to God and ask Him to take it away from you, and to grant you His peace. He wants you to be joyful, and to be at peace.

THE TENTH COMMANDMENT

You shall not covet your neighbor's goods.

It is easy to want things that we don't have, because we think they will make us happy. God reminds us to be happy with what we have. He tells us to not desire the things that belong to others, even if they seem very attractive to us.

The truth is, your greatest treasure is inside you, in your heart. You are a beloved son or daughter of God! Your Heavenly Father lives in your heart by the power of His Holy Spirit. Your heart is good, and you matter very much to God. He wants to draw you closer to Himself, and to fill you with His love. Then He wants to love and serve other people through you. He has given you special gifts that He wants you to share with other people.

All of this takes time. As a child, take your time to play and to enjoy the beautiful world God has made for you. Take your time to learn about all that God has created. Take your time to love others and to be kind to them. God has many wonderful surprises waiting for you as you follow Him and obey His commandments. Jesus said that we are His friends if we do what He commands us. Jesus commands us to love one another, as He has loved us.

THE TWO GREAT COMMANDMENTS

Jesus taught us that the Ten Commandments could actually be summed up in two Great Commandments: "You shall love the Lord your God with all your heart, with all your soul, with all your mind, and with all your strength." He continued, "You shall love your neighbor as yourself." Jesus ended by saying, "There are no other commandments greater than these."

God gave us His Commandments because He wants all of us to live with Him forever in heaven. We show our love for God and others by living as God wants us to live. Ask Jesus in Holy Communion to help you obey God and to love with His love. Let us please God. Let us keep His Commandments!